Ruff and Me

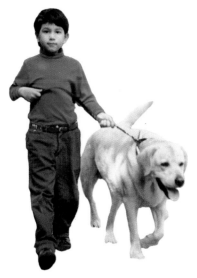

by Karen Anderson

photographs by Wendy Rivers

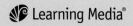 Learning Media®

Here are my eyes.

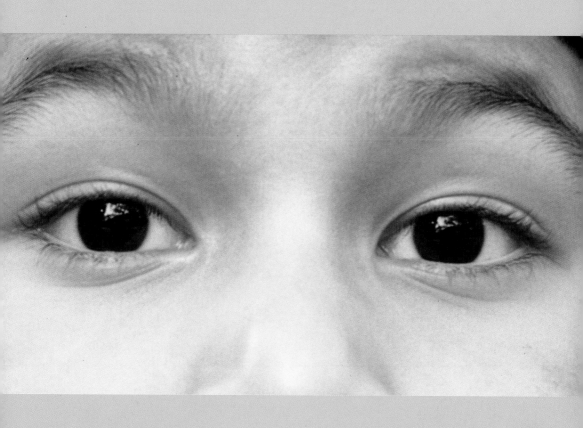

3

Here are Ruff's eyes.

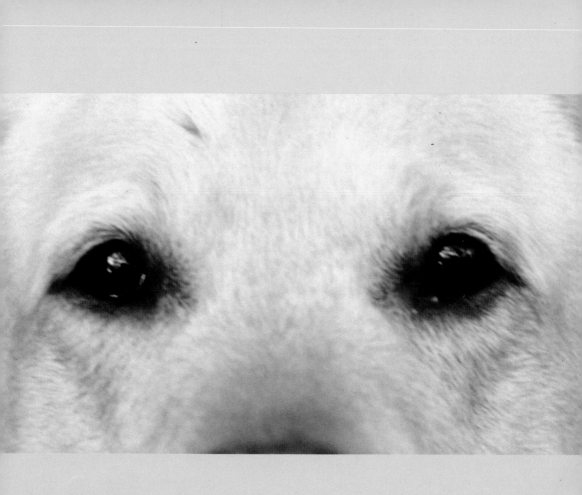

Here are my ears.

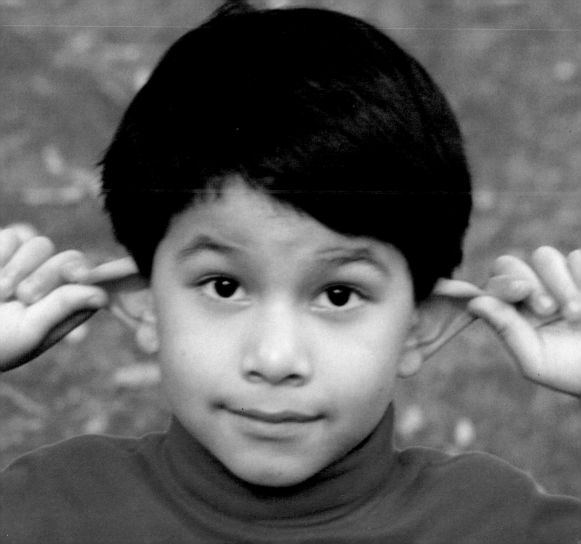

Here are Ruff's ears.

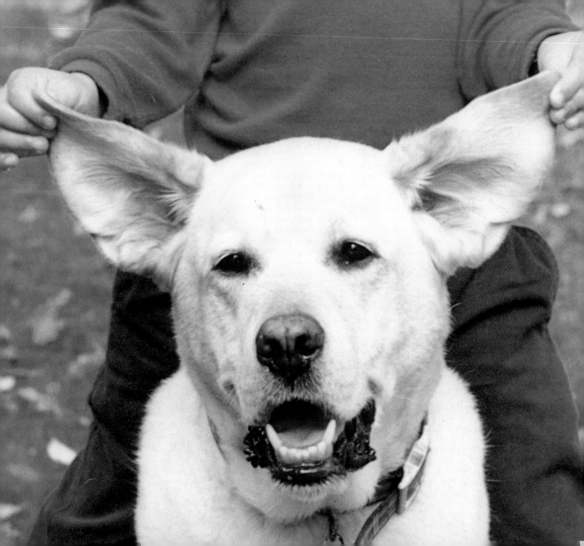

Here are my teeth.

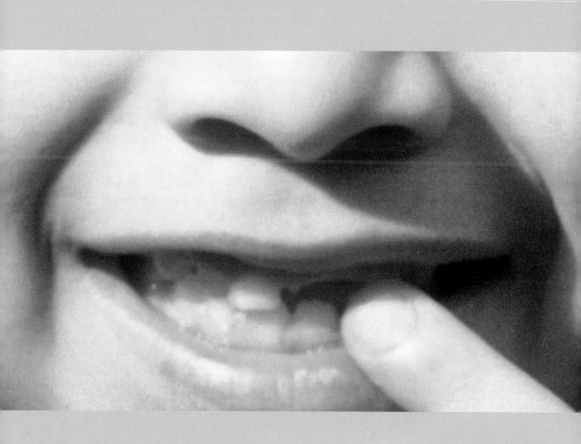

Here are Ruff's teeth.

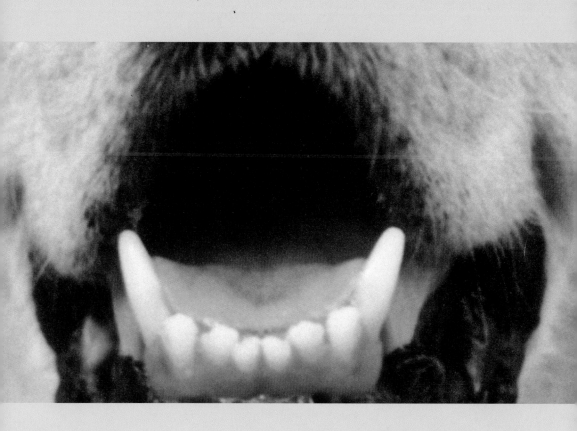

Here I am.

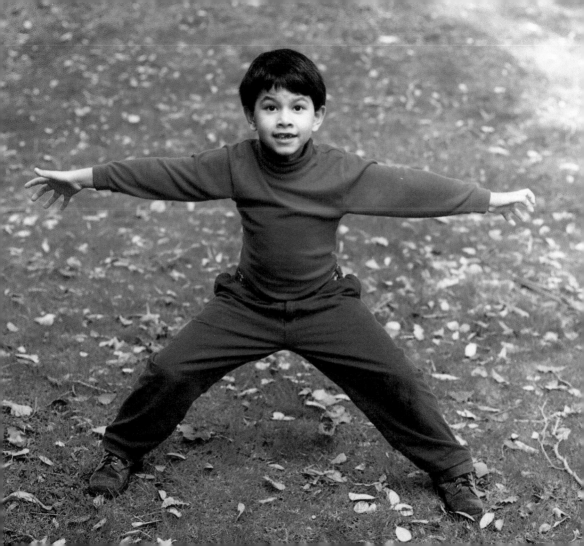

Here we are.

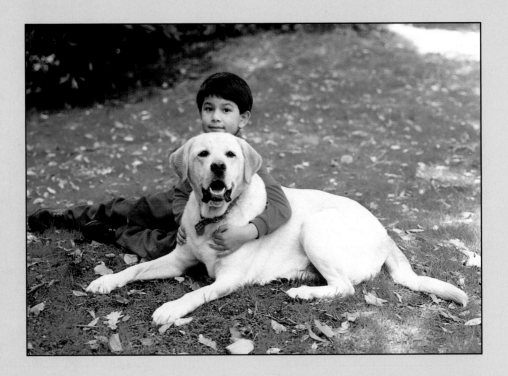